ETHICS IN COMMUNICATIONS

Pontifical Council for
Social Communications

BOOKS & MEDIA
BOSTON

ISBN 0-8198-2349-X

Vatican Translation

Printed and published in the U.S.A. by Pauline Books & Media, 50 Saint Pauls Avenue, Boston MA 02130-3491.

www.pauline.org

Pauline Books & Media is the publishing house of the Daughters of St. Paul, an international congregation of women religious serving the Church with the communications media.

1 2 3 4 5 6 7 05 04 03 02 01 00

Contents

I

Introduction

1. Great good and great evil come from the use people make of the media of social communication. Although it typically is said—and we often shall say here—that "media" do this or that, these are not blind forces of nature beyond human control. For even though acts of communicating often do have unintended consequences, nevertheless, people choose whether to use the media for good or evil ends, in a good or evil way.

These choices, central to the ethical question, are made not only by those who receive communication—viewers, listeners, readers—but especially by those who control the instruments of social communication and determine their structures, policies and content. They include public officials and corporate executives, members of governing boards, owners, publishers and station managers, editors, news directors, producers, writers, correspondents and others. For them, the ethical question is particularly acute: Are the media being used for good or evil?

2. The impact of social communication can hardly be exaggerated. Here people come into contact with other people and with events, form their opinions and values. Not only do they transmit and receive information and ideas through these instru-

ments, but often they experience living itself as an experience of media (cf. Pontifical Council for Social Communications, *Aetatis Novae,* 2).

Technological change rapidly is making the media of communication even more pervasive and powerful. "The advent of the information society is a real cultural revolution" (Pontifical Council for Culture, *Toward a Pastoral Approach to Culture,* 9); and the twentieth century's dazzling innovations may have been only a prologue to what this new century will bring.

The range and diversity of media accessible to people in well-to-do countries already are astonishing: books and periodicals, television and radio, films and videos, audio recordings, electronic communication transmitted over the airwaves, over cable and satellite, via the Internet. The contents of this vast outpouring range from hard news to pure entertainment, prayer to pornography, contemplation to violence. Depending on how they use media, people can grow in sympathy and compassion or become isolated in a narcissistic, self-referential world of stimuli with near-narcotic effects. Not even those who shun the media can avoid contact with others who are deeply influenced by them.

3. Along with these reasons, the Church has reasons of her own for being interested in the means of social communication. Viewed in the light of faith, the history of human communication can be seen as a long journey from Babel, site and symbol of communication's collapse (cf. Gn 11:4–8), to Pentecost and the gift of tongues (cf. Acts 2:5–11)—communication restored by the power of the Spirit sent by the Son. Sent forth into the world to announce the Good News (cf. Mt 28:19–20; Mk 16:15),

the Church has the mission of proclaiming the Gospel until the end of time. Today, she knows, that requires using media (cf. Vatican Council II, *Inter Mirifica,* 3; Pope Paul VI, *Evangelii Nuntiandi,* 45; Pope John Paul II, *Redemptoris Missio,* 37; Pontifical Council for Social Communications, *Communio et Progressio,* 126–134, *Aetatis Novae,* 11).

The Church also knows herself to be a *communio,* a communion of persons and Eucharistic communities, "rooted in and mirroring the intimate communion of the Trinity" (*Aetatis Novae,* 10; cf. Congregation for the Doctrine of the Faith, *Some Aspects of the Church Understood As Communion*). Indeed, all human communication is grounded in the communication among Father, Son and Spirit. But more than that, Trinitarian communion reaches out to humankind: the Son is the Word, eternally "spoken" by the Father; and in and through Jesus Christ, Son and Word made flesh, God communicates himself and his salvation to women and men. "In many and various ways God spoke of old to our fathers by the prophets, but in these last days he has spoken to us by a Son" (Heb 1:1–2). Communication in and by the Church finds its starting point in the communion of love among the divine Persons and their communication with us.

4. The Church's approach to the means of social communication is fundamentally positive, encouraging. She does not simply stand in judgment and condemn; rather, she considers these instruments to be not only products of human genius but also great gifts of God and true signs of the times (cf. *Inter Mirifica,* 1; *Evangelii Nuntiandi,* 45; *Redemptoris Missio,* 37). She desires to support those who are professionally involved in

communication by setting out positive principles to assist them in their work, while fostering a dialogue in which all interested parties—today, that means nearly everyone—can participate. These purposes underlie the present document.

We say again: the media do nothing by themselves; they are instruments, tools, used as people choose to use them. In reflecting upon the means of social communication, we must face honestly the "most essential" question raised by technological progress: whether, as a result of it, the human person "is becoming truly better, that is to say more mature spiritually, more aware of the dignity of his humanity, more responsible, more open to others, especially the neediest and the weakest, and readier to give and to aid all" (Pope John Paul II, *Redemptor Hominis,* 15).

We take it for granted that the vast majority of people involved in social communication in any capacity are conscientious individuals who want to do the right thing. Public officials, policy makers and corporate executives desire to respect and promote the public interest as they understand it. Readers and listeners and viewers want to use their time well for personal growth and development so that they can lead happier, more productive lives. Parents are anxious that what enters their homes through media be in their children's interests. Most professional communicators desire to use their talents to serve the human family, and are troubled by the growing economic and ideological pressures present in many sectors of the media to lower ethical standards.

The contents of the countless choices made by all these people concerning the media are different from group to group and individual to individual, but the choices all have ethical weight and are subject to ethical evaluation. To choose rightly, those choosing need to "know the principles of the moral order and apply them faithfully" (*Inter Mirifica,* 4).

5. The Church brings several things to this conversation. She brings a long tradition of moral wisdom, rooted in divine revelation and human reflection (cf. Pope John Paul II, *Fides et Ratio,* 36–48). Part of this is a substantial and growing body of social teaching, whose theological orientation is an important corrective to "the 'atheistic' solution, which deprives man of one of his basic dimensions, namely the spiritual one, and to permissive and consumerist solutions, which under various pretexts seek to convince man that he is free from every law and from God himself" (Pope John Paul II, *Centesimus Annus,* 55). More than simply passing judgment, this tradition offers itself in service to the media. For example, "the Church's culture of wisdom can save the media culture of information from becoming a meaningless accumulation of facts" (Pope John Paul II, *Message for the 33rd World Communications Day,* 1999).

The Church also brings something else to the conversation. Her special contribution to human affairs, including the world of social communication, is "precisely her vision of the dignity of the person revealed in all its fullness in the mystery of the incarnate Word" (*Centesimus Annus,* 47) In the words of the Second Vatican Council, "Christ the Lord, Christ the new Adam, in the very revelation of the mystery of the Father and of his love, fully reveals man to himself and brings to light his most high calling" (*Gaudium et Spes,* 22).

II

Social Communication That Serves the Human Person

6. Following the Council's Pastoral Constitution on the Church in the Modern World *Gaudium et Spes* (cf. nos.30–31), the Pastoral Instruction on Social Communications *Communio et Progressio* makes it clear that the media are called to serve human dignity by helping people live well and function as persons in community. Media do this by encouraging men and women to be conscious of their dignity, enter into the thoughts and feelings of others, cultivate a sense of mutual responsibility, and grow in personal freedom, in respect for others' freedom, and in the capacity for dialogue.

Social communication has immense power to promote human happiness and fulfillment. Without pretending to do more than give an overview, we note here, as we have done elsewhere (cf. Pontifical Council for Social Communications, *Ethics in Advertising,* 4–8), some economic, political, cultural, educational and religious benefits.

7. *Economic.* The market is not a norm of morality or a source of moral value, and market economics can be abused, but the market can serve the person (cf. *Centesimus Annus,* 34), and media play an indispensable role in a market economy.

Social communication supports business and commerce, helps spur economic growth, employment and prosperity, encourages improvements in the quality of existing goods and services and the development of new ones, fosters responsible competition that serves the public interest, and enables people to make informed choices by telling them about the availability and features of products.

In short, today's complex national and international economic systems could not function without the media. Remove them, and crucial economic structures would collapse, with great harm to countless people and to society.

8. *Political.* Social communication benefits society by facilitating informed citizen participation in the political process. The media draw people together for the pursuit of shared purposes and goals, thus helping to form and sustain authentic political communities.

Media are indispensable in today's democratic societies. They supply information about issues and events, officeholders and candidates for office. They enable leaders to communicate quickly and directly with the public about urgent matters. They are important instruments of accountability, turning the spotlight on incompetence, corruption and abuses of trust, while also calling attention to instances of competence, public-spiritedness and devotion to duty.

9. *Cultural.* The means of social communication offer people access to literature, drama, music and art otherwise unavailable to them, and so promote human development in respect to knowledge and wisdom and beauty. We speak not only of presentations of classic works and the fruits of scholarship, but also of wholesome popular entertainment and useful

information that draw families together, help people solve everyday problems, raise the spirits of the sick, shut-ins and the elderly, and relieve the tedium of life.

Media also make it possible for ethnic groups to cherish and celebrate their cultural traditions, share them with others, and transmit them to new generations. In particular, they introduce children and young people to their cultural heritage. Communicators, like artists, serve the common good by preserving and enriching the cultural heritage of nations and peoples (cf. Pope John Paul II, *Letter to Artists,* 4).

10. *Educational.* The media are important tools of education in many contexts, from school to workplace, and at many stages in life. Preschoolers being introduced to the rudiments of reading and mathematics, young people seeking vocational training or degrees, elderly persons pursuing new learning in their latter years—these and many others have access via these means to a rich and growing panoply of educational resources.

Media are standard instructional tools in many classrooms. And beyond the classroom walls, the instruments of communication, including the Internet, conquer barriers of distance and isolation, bringing learning opportunities to villagers in remote areas, cloistered religious, the homebound, prisoners and many others.

11. *Religious.* Many people's religious lives are greatly enriched through the media. They carry news and information about religious events, ideas and personalities; they serve as vehicles for evangelization and catechesis. Day in and day out, they provide inspiration, encouragement and opportunities for worship to persons confined to their homes or to institutions.

Sometimes, too, media contribute to people's spiritual enrichment in extraordinary ways. For example, huge audiences around the world view and, in a sense, participate in important events in the life of the Church that are regularly telecast via satellite from Rome. And over the years, media have brought the words and images of the Holy Father's pastoral visits to countless millions.

12. In all these settings—economic, political, cultural, educational, religious—as well as others, the media can be used to build and sustain human community. And indeed all communication ought to be open to community among persons.

"In order to become brothers and sisters, it is necessary to know one another. To do this, it is...important to communicate more extensively and more deeply" (Congregation for Institutes of Consecrated Life and Societies of Apostolic Life, *Fraternal Life in Community,* 29). Communication that serves genuine community is "more than the expression of ideas and the indication of emotion. At its most profound level, it is the giving of self in love" (*Communio et Progressio,* 11).

Communication like this seeks the well-being and fulfillment of community members in respect to the common good of all. But consultation and dialogue are needed to discern this common good. Therefore it is imperative for the parties to social communication to engage in such dialogue and submit themselves to the truth about what is good. This is how the media can meet their obligation to "witness to the truth about life, about human dignity, about the true meaning of our freedom and mutual interdependence" (Pope John Paul II, *Message for the 33rd World Communications Day,* 1999).

III

Social Communication That Violates the Good of the Person

13. The media also can be used to block community and injure the integral good of persons: by alienating people or marginalizing and isolating them; drawing them into perverse communities organized around false, destructive values; fostering hostility and conflict, demonizing others and creating a mentality of "us" against "them"; presenting what is base and degrading in a glamorous light, while ignoring or belittling what uplifts and ennobles; spreading misinformation and disinformation, fostering trivialization and banality. Stereotyping—based on race and ethnicity, sex, age and other factors, including religion—is distressingly common in media. Often, too, social communication overlooks what is genuinely new and important, including the good news of the Gospel, and concentrates on the fashionable or faddish.

Abuses exist in each of the areas just mentioned.

14. *Economic*. The media sometimes are used to build and sustain economic systems that serve acquisitiveness and greed. Neoliberalism is a case in point: "Based on a purely economic conception of man," it "considers profit and the law of the

market as its only parameters, to the detriment of the dignity of and the respect due to individuals and peoples" (Pope John Paul II, *Ecclesia in America,* 156). In such circumstances, means of communication that ought to benefit all are exploited for the advantage of the few.

The process of globalization "can create unusual opportunities for greater prosperity" (*Centesimus Annus,* 58); but side by side with it, and even as part of it, some nations and peoples suffer exploitation and marginalization, falling further and further behind in the struggle for development. These expanding pockets of privation in the midst of plenty are seedbeds of envy, resentment, tension and conflict. This underlines the need for "effective international agencies which will oversee and direct the economy to the common good" (*Centesimus Annus,* 58).

Faced with grave injustices, it is not enough for communicators simply to say that their job is to report things as they are. That undoubtedly is their job. But some instances of human suffering are largely ignored by media even as others are reported, and insofar as this reflects a decision by communicators, it reflects indefensible selectivity. Even more fundamentally, communication structures and policies and the allocation of technology are factors helping to make some people "information rich" and others "information poor" at a time when prosperity, and even survival, depend on information.

In such ways, then, media often contribute to the injustices and imbalances that give rise to suffering they report. "It is necessary to break down the barriers and monopolies which leave so many countries on the margins of development, and to provide all individuals and nations with the basic conditions which will enable them to share in development" (*Centesimus Annus,* 35). Communications and information technology, along with training in its use, is one such basic condition.

15. *Political.* Unscrupulous politicians use media for demagoguery and deception in support of unjust policies and oppressive regimes. They misrepresent opponents and systematically distort and suppress the truth by propaganda and "spin." Rather than drawing people together, media then serve to drive them apart, creating tensions and suspicions that set the stage for conflict.

Even in countries with democratic systems, it is all too common for political leaders to manipulate public opinion through the media instead of fostering informed participation in the political process. The conventions of democracy are observed, but techniques borrowed from advertising and public relations are deployed on behalf of policies that exploit particular groups and violate fundamental rights, including the right to life (cf. Pope John Paul II, *Evangelium Vitae,* 70).

Often, too, the media popularize the ethical relativism and utilitarianism that underlie today's culture of death. They participate in the contemporary "conspiracy against life" by "lending credit to that culture which presents recourse to contraception, sterilization, abortion and even euthanasia as a mark of progress and a victory of freedom, while depicting as enemies of freedom and progress those positions which are unreservedly pro-life" (*Evangelium Vitae,* 17).

16. *Cultural.* Critics frequently decry the superficiality and bad taste of media, and although they are not obliged to be somber and dull, they should not be tawdry and demeaning

either. It is no excuse to say the media reflect popular standards, for they also powerfully influence popular standards and so have a serious duty to uplift, not degrade, them.

The problem takes various forms. Instead of explaining complex matters carefully and truthfully, news media avoid or oversimplify them. Entertainment media feature presentations of a corrupting, dehumanizing kind, including exploitative treatments of sexuality and violence. It is grossly irresponsible to ignore or dismiss the fact that "pornography and sadistic violence debase sexuality, corrode human relationships, exploit individuals—especially women and young people, undermine marriage and family life, foster anti-social behavior and weaken the moral fiber of society itself" (Pontifical Council for Social Communications, *Pornography and Violence in the Communications Media: A Pastoral Response*, 10).

On the international level, cultural domination imposed through the means of social communication also is a serious, growing problem. Traditional cultural expressions are virtually excluded from access to popular media in some places and face extinction; meanwhile the values of affluent, secularized societies increasingly supplant the traditional values of societies less wealthy and powerful. In considering these matters, particular attention should go to providing children and young people with media presentations that put them in living contact with their cultural heritage.

Communication across cultural lines is desirable. Societies can and should learn from one another. But transcultural communication should not be at the expense of the less powerful. Today "even the least widespread cultures are no longer isolated. They benefit from an increase in contacts, but they also suffer from the pressures of a powerful trend toward uniformity" (*Toward a Pastoral Approach to Culture,* 33). That so much communication now flows in one direction only—from developed nations to the developing and the poor—raises serious ethical questions. Have the rich nothing to learn from the poor? Are the powerful deaf to the voices of the weak?

17. *Educational.* Instead of promoting learning, media can distract people and cause them to waste time. Children and young people are especially harmed in this way, but adults also suffer from exposure to banal, trashy presentations. Among the causes of this abuse of trust by communicators is greed that puts profits before persons.

Sometimes, too, media are used as tools of indoctrination, with the aim of controlling what people know and denying them access to information the authorities do not want them to have. This is a perversion of genuine education, which seeks to expand people's knowledge and skills and help them pursue worthy purposes, not narrow their horizons and harness their energies in the service of ideology.

18. *Religious.* In the relationship between the means of social communication and religion there are temptations on both sides.

On the side of the media, these include ignoring or marginalizing religious ideas and experience; treating religion with incomprehension, perhaps even contempt, as an object of curiosity that does not merit serious attention; promoting religious fads at the expense of traditional faith; treating legitimate religious groups with hostility; weighing religion and religious experience by secular standards of what is appropriate, and favoring religious views that conform to secular tastes over those that do not; trying to imprison transcendence within the confines of rationalism and skepticism. Today's media often mirror the postmodern state of a human spirit "locked within the confines of its own immanence without reference of any kind to the transcendent" (*Fides et Ratio,* 81).

The temptations on the side of religion include taking an exclusively judgmental and negative view of media; failing to understand that reasonable standards of good media practice, such as objectivity and even-handedness, may preclude special treatment for religion's institutional interests; presenting religious messages in an emotional, manipulative style, as if they were products competing in a glutted marketplace; using media as instruments for control and domination; practicing unnecessary secrecy and otherwise offending against truth; downplaying the Gospel's demand for conversion, repentance and amendment of life, while substituting a bland religiosity that asks little of people; encouraging fundamentalism, fanaticism and religious exclusivism that foment disdain and hostility toward others.

19. In short, the media can be used for good or for evil—it is a matter of choice. "It can never be forgotten that communication through the media is not a utilitarian exercise intended simply to motivate, persuade or sell. Still less is it a vehicle for ideology. The media can at times reduce human beings to units of consumption or competing interest groups, or manipulate viewers, readers and listeners as mere ciphers from whom some advantage is sought, whether product sales or political support, and these things destroy community. It is

the task of communication to bring people together and enrich their lives, not isolate and exploit them. The means of social communication, properly used, can help to create and sustain a human community based on justice and charity, and, in so far as they do that, they will be signs of hope" (Pope John Paul II, *Message for the 32nd World Communications Day,* 1998).

IV

Some Relevant Ethical Principles

20. Ethical principles and norms relevant in other fields also apply to social communication. Principles of social ethics like solidarity, subsidiarity, justice, equity and accountability in the use of public resources and the performance of roles of public trust are always applicable. Communication must always be truthful, since truth is essential to individual liberty and to authentic community among persons.

Ethics in social communication is concerned not just with what appears on cinema and television screens, on radio broadcasts, on the printed page and the Internet, but with a great deal else besides. The ethical dimension relates not just to the content of communication (the message) and the process of communication (how the communicating is done), but to fundamental structural and systemic issues, often involving large questions of policy bearing upon the distribution of sophisticated technology and product (who shall be information rich and who shall be information poor?). These questions point to other questions with economic and political implications for ownership and control. At least in open societies with market economies, the largest ethical question of all may be how to balance profit against service to the public interest understood according to an inclusive conception of the common good.

Even to reasonable people of good will, it is not always immediately clear how to apply ethical principles and norms to particular cases; reflection, discussion and dialogue are needed. We offer what follows with the hope of encouraging such reflection and dialogue—among communication policy makers, professional communicators, ethicists and moralists, recipients of communication, and others concerned.

21. In all three areas—message, process, structural and systemic issues—the fundamental ethical principle is this: the human person and the human community are the end and measure of the use of the media of social communication; communication should be by persons to persons for the integral development of persons.

Integral development requires a sufficiency of material goods and products, but it also requires attention to the "inner dimension" (*Sollicitudo Rei Socialis,* 29; cf. 46). Everyone deserves the opportunity to grow and flourish in respect to the full range of physical, intellectual, emotional, moral and spiritual goods. Individuals have irreducible dignity and importance, and may never be sacrificed to collective interests.

22. A second principle is complementary to the first: the good of persons cannot be realized apart from the common good of the communities to which they belong. This common good should be understood in inclusive terms, as the sum total of worthy shared purposes to whose pursuit community members jointly commit themselves and which the community exists to serve.

Thus, while social communication rightly looks to the needs and interests of particular groups, it should not do so in a way that sets one group against another—for example, in the name of class conflict, exaggerated nationalism, racial supremacy, ethnic cleansing and the like. The virtue of solidarity, "a firm and persevering determination to commit oneself to the common good" (*Sollicitudo Rei Socialis,* 38), ought to govern all areas of social life—economic, political, cultural, religious.

Communicators and communication policy makers must serve the real needs and interests both of individuals and of groups, at all levels and of all kinds. There is a pressing need for equity at the international level, where the maldistribution of material goods between North and South is exacerbated by a maldistribution of communication resources and information technology, upon which productivity and prosperity greatly depend. Similar problems also exist within wealthy countries, "where the constant transformation of the methods of production and consumption devalues certain acquired skills and professional expertise" and "those who fail to keep up with the times can easily be marginalized" (*Centesimus Annus,* 33).

Clearly, then, there is a need for broad participation in making decisions not only about the messages and processes of social communication but also about systemic issues and the allocation of resources. The decision makers have a serious moral duty to recognize the needs and interests of those who are particularly vulnerable—the poor, the elderly and unborn, children and youth, the oppressed and marginalized, women and minorities, the sick and disabled—as well as families and religious groups. Today especially, the international community and international communications interests should take a generous and inclusive approach to nations and regions where what the means of social communication do—or fail to do—bears a share of the blame for the perpetuation of evils like poverty, illiteracy, political repression and violations of human rights, intergroup and interreligious conflicts and the suppression of indigenous cultures.

23. Even so, we continue to believe that "the solution to problems arising from unregulated commercialization and privatization does not lie in state control of media but in more regulation according to criteria of public service and in greater public accountability. It should be noted in this connection that, although the legal and political frameworks within which media operate in some countries are currently changing strikingly for the better, elsewhere government intervention remains an instrument of oppression and exclusion" (*Aetatis Novae,* 5).

The presumption should always be in favor of freedom of expression, for "when people follow their natural inclination to exchange ideas and declare their opinions, they are not merely making use of a right. They are also performing a social duty" (*Communio et Progressio,* 45). Still, considered from an ethical perspective, this presumption is not an absolute, indefeasible norm. There are obvious instances—for example, libel and slander, messages that seek to foster hatred and conflict among individuals and groups, obscenity and pornography, the morbid depiction of violence—where no right to communicate exists. Plainly, too, free expression should always observe principles like truth, fairness and respect for privacy.

Professional communicators should be actively involved in developing and enforcing ethical codes of behavior for their profession, in cooperation with public representatives. Religious bodies and other groups likewise deserve to be part of this continuing effort.

24. Another relevant principle, already mentioned, concerns public participation in making decisions about communications policy. At all levels, this participation should be organized, systematic and genuinely representative, not skewed in favor of particular groups. This principle applies even, and perhaps especially, where media are privately owned and operated for profit.

In the interests of public participation, communicators "must seek to communicate with people, and not just speak to them. This involves learning about people's needs, being aware of their struggles and presenting all forms of communication with the sensitivity that human dignity requires" (Pope John Paul II, *Address to Communications Specialists,* Los Angeles, September 15, 1987).

Circulation, broadcast ratings and "box office," along with market research, are sometimes said to be the best indicators of public sentiment—in fact, the only ones necessary for the law of the market to operate. No doubt the market's voice can be heard in these ways. But decisions about media content and policy should not be left only to the market and to economic factors—profits—since these cannot be counted on to safeguard either the public interest as a whole or, especially, the legitimate interests of minorities.

To some extent, this objection may be answered by the concept of the "niche," according to which particular periodicals, programs, stations and channels are directed to particular audiences. The approach is legitimate, up to a point. But diversification and specialization—organizing media to correspond to audiences broken down into ever-smaller units based largely on economic factors and patterns of consumption—should not be carried too far. Media of social communication must remain an "Areopagus" (cf. *Redemptoris Missio,* 37)—a forum for exchanging ideas and information, drawing individuals and groups together, fostering solidarity and peace. The Internet in particular raises concerns about some of the "radically new consequences it brings: a loss of the intrinsic value of items of information, an undifferentiated uniformity in messages that are reduced to pure information, a lack of responsible feedback and a certain discouragement of interpersonal relationships" (*Toward a Pastoral Approach to Culture,* 9).

25. Professional communicators are not the only ones with ethical duties. Audiences—recipients—have obligations too. Communicators attempting to meet their responsibilities deserve audiences conscientious about theirs.

The first duty of recipients of social communication is to be discerning and selective. They should inform themselves about media—their structures, mode of operation, contents—and make responsible choices, according to ethically sound criteria, about what to read or watch or listen to. Today everybody needs some form of continuing media education, whether by personal study or participation in an organized program or both. More than just teaching about techniques, media education helps people form standards of good taste and truthful moral judgment, an aspect of conscience formation.

Through her schools and formation programs the Church should provide media education of this kind (cf. *Aetatis Novae,* 28; *Communio et Progressio,* 107). Directed originally to institutes of consecrated life, the following words have a broader application: "A community, aware of the influence of the media, should learn to use them for personal and community growth, with the evangelical clarity and inner freedom of those who have learned to know Christ (cf. Gal 4:17–23). The media propose, and often impose, a mentality and model of life in constant contrast with the Gospel. In this connection, in many areas one hears of the desire for deeper formation in receiving and using the media, both critically and fruitfully" (Congregation for Institutes of Consecrated Life and Societies of Apostolic Life, *Fraternal Life in Community,* 34).

Similarly, parents have a serious duty to help their children learn how to evaluate and use the media, by forming their consciences correctly and developing their critical faculties (cf. *Familiaris Consortio,* 76). For their children's sake, as well as their own, parents must learn and practice the skills of discerning viewers and listeners and readers, acting as models of prudent use of media in the home. According to their age and circumstances, children and young people should be open to formation regarding media, resisting the easy path of uncritical passivity, peer pressure and commercial exploitation. Families—parents and children together—will find it helpful to come together in groups to study and discuss the problems and opportunities created by social communication.

26. Besides promoting media education, the institutions, agencies and programs of the Church have other important responsibilities in regard to social communication. First and foremost, the Church's practice of communication should be exemplary, reflecting the highest standards of truthfulness, accountability, sensitivity to human rights, and other relevant

principles and norms. Beyond that, the Church's own media should be committed to communicating the fullness of the truth about the meaning of human life and history, especially as it is contained in God's revealed word and expressed by the teaching of the Magisterium. Pastors should encourage use of media to spread the Gospel (cf. *Code of Canon Law,* Canon 822.1).

Those who represent the Church must be honest and straightforward in their relations with journalists. Even though the questions they ask are "sometimes embarrassing or disappointing, especially when they in no way correspond to the message we have to get across," one must bear in mind that "these disconcerting questions are often asked by most of our contemporaries" (*Toward a Pastoral Approach to Culture,* 34). For the Church to speak credibly to people today, those who speak for her have to give credible, truthful answers to these seemingly awkward questions.

Catholics, like other citizens, have the right of free expression, including the right of access to the media for this purpose. The right of expression includes expressing opinions about the good of the Church, with due regard for the integrity of faith and morals, respect for the pastors, and consideration for the common good and the dignity of persons (cf. Canon 212.3; Canon 227). No one, however, has a right to speak for the Church, or imply he or she does, unless properly designated, and personal opinions should not be presented as the Church's teaching (cf. Canon 227).

The Church would be well served if more of those who hold offices and perform functions in her name received communication training. This is true not only of seminarians, persons in formation in religious communities and young lay

Catholics, but Church personnel generally. Provided the media are "neutral, open and honest," they offer well-prepared Christians "a frontline missionary role" and it is important that the latter be "well-trained and supported." Pastors also should offer their people guidance regarding media and their sometimes discordant and even destructive messages (cf. Canon 822.2, 3).

Similar considerations apply to internal communication in the Church. A two-way flow of information and views between pastors and faithful, freedom of expression sensitive to the well-being of the community and to the role of the Magisterium in fostering it, and responsible public opinion all are important expressions of "the fundamental right of dialogue and information within the Church" (*Aetatis Novae,* 10; cf. *Communio et Progressio,* 20).

The right of expression must be exercised with deference to revealed truth and the Church's teaching, and with respect for others' ecclesial rights (cf. Canon 212.1, 2, 3, Canon 220). Like other communities and institutions, the Church sometimes needs—in fact, is sometimes obliged—to practice secrecy and confidentiality. But this should not be for the sake of manipulation and control. Within the communion of faith, "holders of office, who are invested with a sacred power, are in fact dedicated to promoting the interests of their brethren, so that all who belong to the People of God, and are consequently endowed with true Christian dignity, may through their free and well-ordered efforts toward a common good, attain to salvation" (*Lumen Gentium,* 18). Right practice in communication is one of the ways of realizing this vision.

V

Conclusion

27. As the third millennium of the Christian era begins, humankind is well along in creating a global network for the instantaneous transmission of information, ideas and value judgments in science, commerce, education, entertainment, politics, the arts, religion and every other field.

This network already is directly accessible to many people in their homes, schools and workplaces—indeed, wherever they may be. It is commonplace to view events, from sports to wars, happening in real time on the other side of the planet. People can tap directly into quantities of data beyond the reach of many scholars and students just a short time ago. An individual can ascend to heights of human genius and virtue, or plunge to the depths of human degradation, while sitting alone at a keyboard and screen. Communication technology constantly achieves new breakthroughs, with enormous potential for good and ill. As interactivity increases, the distinction between communicators and recipients blurs. Continuing research is needed into the impact, and especially the ethical implications, of new and emerging media.

28. But despite their immense power, the means of communication are, and will remain, only media—that is to say: instru-

ments, tools, available for both good and evil uses. The choice is ours. The media do not call for a new ethic; they call for the application of established principles to new circumstances. And this is a task in which everyone has a role to play. Ethics in the media is not the business only of specialists, whether they be specialists in social communication or specialists in moral philosophy; rather, the reflection and dialogue that this document seeks to encourage and assist must be broad and inclusive.

29. Social communication can join people in communities of sympathy and shared interest. Will these communities be informed by justice, decency and respect for human rights; will they be committed to the common good? Or will they be selfish and inward-looking, committed to the benefit of particular groups—economic, racial, political, even religious—at others' expense? Will new technology serve all nations and peoples, while respecting the cultural traditions of each, or will it be a tool to enrich the rich and empower the powerful? We have to choose.

The means of communication also can be used to separate and isolate. More and more, technology allows people to assemble packages of information and services uniquely designed for them. There are real advantages in that, but it raises an inescapable question: Will the audience of the future be a multitude of audiences of one? While the new technology can enhance individual autonomy, it has other, less desirable implications. Instead of being a global community, might the "web" of the future turn out to be a vast, fragmented network of isolated individuals—human bees in their cells—interacting with data instead of with one another? What would become of solidarity—what would become of love—in a world like that?

In the best of circumstances, human communication has

serious limitations, is more or less imperfect and in danger of failing. It is hard for people consistently to communicate honestly with one another, in a way that does no harm and serves the best interests of all. In the world of media, moreover, the inherent difficulties of communicating often are magnified by ideology, by the desire for profit and political control, by rivalries and conflicts between groups, and by other social ills. Today's media vastly increase the outreach of social communication—its quantity, its speed; they do not make the reaching out of mind to mind and heart to heart any less fragile, less sensitive, less prone to fail.

30. As we have said, the special contributions which the Church brings to the discussion of these matters are a vision of human persons and their incomparable dignity and inviolable rights, and a vision of human community whose members are joined by the virtue of solidarity in pursuit of the common good of all. The need for these two visions is especially pressing "at a time when we are faced with the patent inadequacy of perspectives in which the ephemeral is affirmed as a value and the possibility of discovering the real meaning of life is cast into doubt"; lacking them, "many people stumble through life to the very edge of the abyss without knowing where they are going" (*Fides et Ratio,* 6).

In the face of this crisis, the Church stands forth as an "expert in humanity" whose expertise "leads her necessarily to extend her religious mission to the various fields" of human endeavor (*Sollicitudo Rei Socialis,* 41; cf. Pope Paul VI, *Populorum Progressio,* 13). She may not keep the truth about the human person and the human community to herself; she must share it freely, always aware that people can say no to the truth—and to her.

Attempting to foster and support high ethical standards in the use of the means of social communication, the Church seeks dialogue and collaboration with others: with public officials, who have a particular duty to protect and promote the common good of the political community; with men and women from the world of culture and the arts; with scholars and teachers engaged in forming the communicators and audiences of the future; with members of other churches and religious groups, who share her desire that media be used for the glory of God and the service of the human race (cf. Pontifical Council for Social Communications, *Criteria for Ecumenical and Interreligious Cooperation in Communications*); and especially with professional communicators—writers, editors, reporters, correspondents, performers, producers, technical personnel—together with owners, administrators and policy makers in this field.

31. Along with its limitations, human communication has in it something of God's creative activity. "With loving regard, the divine Artist passes on to the human artist"—and, we might say, to the communicator as well—"a spark of his own surpassing wisdom, calling him to share in his creative power"; in coming to understand this, artists and communicators "come to a full understanding of themselves, their vocation and their mission" (*Letter to Artists,* 1).

The Christian communicator in particular has a prophetic task, a vocation: to speak out against the false gods and idols of the day—materialism, hedonism, consumerism, narrow nationalism, and the rest—holding up for all to see a body of moral truth based on human dignity and rights, the preferential option for the poor, the universal destination of goods, love of enemies, and unconditional respect for all human life from conception to natural death, and seeking the more perfect realization of the kingdom in this world while remaining aware that, at the end of time, Jesus will restore all things and return them to the Father (cf. 1 Cor 15:24).

32. While these reflections are addressed to all persons of good will, not just Catholics, it is appropriate, in bringing them to a close, to speak of Jesus as a model for communicators. "In these last days" God the Father "has spoken to us by a Son" (Heb 1:2), and this Son communicates to us now and always the Father's love and the ultimate meaning of our lives.

"While he was on earth Christ revealed himself as the perfect communicator. Through his incarnation, he utterly identified himself with those who were to receive his communication, and he gave his message not only in words but in the whole manner of his life. He spoke from within, that is to say, from out of the press of his people. He preached the divine message without fear or compromise. He adjusted to his people's way of talking and to their patterns of thought. And he spoke out of the predicament of their time" (*Communio et Progressio,* 11).

Throughout Jesus' public life crowds flocked to hear him preach and teach (cf. Mt 8:1, 18; Mk 2:2, 4:1; Lk 5:1, etc.), and he taught them "as one who had authority" (Mt 7:29; cf. Mk 1:22; Lk 4:32). He told them about the Father and at the same time referred them to himself, explaining, "I am the way, and the truth, and the life" (Jn 14:6) and "he who has seen me has seen the Father" (Jn 14:9). He did not waste time on idle speech or on vindicating himself, not even when he was accused and condemned (cf. Mt 26:63, 27:12–14; Mk 15:5, 15:61). For his "food" was to do the will of the Father who sent him (Jn 4:34), and all he said and did was spoken and done in reference to that.

Often Jesus' teaching took the form of parables and vivid stories expressing profound truths in simple, everyday terms. Not only his words but his deeds, especially his miracles, were acts of communication, pointing to his identity and manifesting the power of God (cf. *Evangelii Nuntiandi,* 12). In his communications he showed respect for his listeners, sympathy for their situation and needs, compassion for their suffering (e.g., Lk 7:13), and resolute determination to tell them what they needed to hear, in a way that would command their attention and help them receive the message, without coercion or compromise, deception or manipulation. He invited others to open their minds and hearts to him, knowing this was how they would be drawn to him and his Father (e.g., Jn 3:1–15, 4:7–26).

Jesus taught that communication is a moral act: "For out of the abundance of the heart the mouth speaks. The good man out of his good treasure brings forth good, and the evil man out of his evil treasure brings forth evil. I tell you, on the day of judgment men will render an account for every careless word they utter, for by your words you will be justified, and by your words you will be condemned" (Mt 12:34–37). He cautioned sternly against scandalizing the "little ones," and warned that for one who did, "it would be better...if a great millstone were hung round his neck and he were thrown into the sea" (Mk 9:42; cf. Mt 18:6, Lk 17:2). He was altogether candid, a man of whom it could be said that "no guile was found on his lips"; and further: "When he was reviled, he did not revile in return;

when he suffered, he did not threaten, but he trusted to him who judges justly" (1 Pt 2:22–23). He insisted on candor and truthfulness in others, while condemning hypocrisy, dishonesty—any kind of communication that was bent and perverse: "Let what you say be simply 'Yes' or 'No'; anything more than this comes from evil" (Mt 5:37).

33. Jesus is the model and the standard of our communicating. For those involved in social communication, whether as policy makers or professional communicators or recipients or in any other role, the conclusion is clear: "Therefore, putting away falsehood, let everyone speak the truth with his neighbor, for we are members one of another.... Let no evil talk come out of your mouths, but only such as is good for edifying, as fits the occasion, that it may impart grace to those who hear" (Eph 4:25, 29). Serving the human person, building up human community grounded in solidarity, justice and love, and speaking the truth about human life and its final fulfillment in God were, are, and will remain at the heart of ethics in the media.

Vatican City, June 4, 2000, World Communications Day, Jubilee of Journalists.

John P. Foley
President

Pierfranco Pastore
Secretary

The Daughters of St. Paul operate book and media centers at the following addresses. Visit, call or write the one nearest you today, or find us on the World Wide Web, www.pauline.org

California
3908 Sepulveda Blvd., Culver City, CA 90230; 310-397-8676
5945 Balboa Ave., San Diego, CA 92111; 858-565-9181
46 Geary Street, San Francisco, CA 94108; 415-781-5180

Florida
145 S.W. 107th Ave., Miami, FL 33174; 305-559-6715

Hawaii
1143 Bishop Street, Honolulu, HI 96813; 808-521-2731
Neighbor Islands call: 800-259-8463

Illinois
172 North Michigan Ave., Chicago, IL 60601; 312-346-4228

Louisiana
4403 Veterans Memorial Blvd., Metairie, LA 70006; 504-887-7631

Massachusetts
Rte. 1, 885 Providence Hwy., Dedham, MA 02026; 781-326-5385

Missouri
9804 Watson Rd., St. Louis, MO 63126; 314-965-3512

New Jersey
561 U.S. Route 1, Wick Plaza, Edison, NJ 08817; 732-572-1200

New York
150 East 52nd Street, New York, NY 10022; 212-754-1110
78 Fort Place, Staten Island, NY 10301; 718-447-5071

Ohio
2105 Ontario Street, Cleveland, OH 44115; 216-621-9427

Pennsylvania
9171-A Roosevelt Blvd., Philadelphia, PA 19114; 215-676-9494

South Carolina
243 King Street, Charleston, SC 29401; 843-577-0175

Tennessee
4811 Poplar Ave., Memphis, TN 38117; 901-761-2987

Texas
114 Main Plaza, San Antonio, TX 78205; 210-224-8101

Virginia
1025 King Street, Alexandria, VA 22314; 703-549-3806

Canada
3022 Dufferin Street, Toronto, Ontario, Canada M6B 3T5; 416-781-9131
1155 Yonge Street, Toronto, Ontario, Canada M4T 1W2; 416-934-3440

¡También somos su fuente para libros, videos y música en español!